DIY Can Candy & Desserts: Recipes From Around the World

Easy to Follow Recipe Guide for THC infused Candy, Ice-cream, Muffins, Cookies, Brownies & So Much More!

By

Jackie Sanders

Published by:

Valley Of Joy Publishing Press

Cover & Interior Design

By

John Segrest

First Edition

Legal Disclaimer

This book contains information about controlled and illegal substances, especially the plant cannabis and its derivative products. Valley of Joy Publishing Press emphasizes that cannabis and its derivative products are considered controlled substances in the U.S., and throughout most of the world. As such, use of such products where it is against the law is not implied or suggested.

The goal of this book is to educate and to entertain only. Readers should use and enjoy the included suggested ways of preparing Cannabis only where it is legal by law.

CONTENTS

INTRODUCTION

Marijuana, am I right? Regardless of what your main use for this infamous little plant may be, it is always recommended to know where it comes from, what it is used for, the chemical components behind it, and a way to adapt it to your personal preferences.

All throughout this book, we will talk about the various kinds of marijuana plants, their respective effects, how to make tinctures and extracts, and last– but definitely not least– a compilation of recipes for cannabis-related desserts and candy.

But here is the twist: these are not just your typical brownie-and-cookie combinations. We will look at international dessert staples from various countries in the world, all given a cannabis-infused twist.

Without further ado, let's dig right in and start learning more about what we refer to as cannabis, marijuana, Mary Jane, ganja, but it is that green plant that relieves our anxiety and our chronic pain.

MAIN TYPES OF CANNABIS

CANNABIS SATIVA

Let's talk about the Sativa strain, our first eligible bachelor. That strain leads to more creative, energetic results– but remember it also varies from person to person, and their own individual chemistry, so one particular reaction is not always guaranteed.

Sativa can be identified through the spiky ridges on the side of its eight leaves, and on the length of time, it takes for it to flower, which is typically longer than other strains. Despite that fact, it still is an old classic amongst regular smokers and marijuana consumers.

CANNABIS INDICA

Now for the runt out of the two widely-known strains: Cannabis Indica. About half the height of Sativa and featuring rounded leaves, this resinous strain is for the type of individual who struggles to sleep. Whether it is migraines, anxiety, insomnia, or overall aching chronic pain, Indica is said to relieve all of those ailments with its soothing properties.

Here is a stranger from the North. Now, what this means is that the next strain is one not many people have heard much about. Cannabis Ruderalis tends to flower quicker than the previous strains we just mentioned.

Because of its fascinating affinity to the cold and its fast-growing characteristics, it is mostly utilized in cross-breeding with other types of strains. The resulting marijuana plant will not wilt if it is grown in northern regions of the world, having an automatic resistance to colder climates.

INDUSTRIAL HEMP

The third variety of Cannabis is called industrial hemp. It branches off from Sativa, or the first strain we covered earlier in previous pages. There are three main factors that make this plant more desirable than other breeds: resistance to pests, uncannily quick growth speed, and rich, fibrous content.

As a result of these characteristics, hemp is regularly harnessed into clothing or textiles, biofuel, paper, paint, and so many more day-to-day items. Next time you are searching for a biodegradable alternative to certain objects or an eco-friendly notebook, you will be pleasantly surprised in the quality of hemp-based products.

HYBRIDS

Hybrids are made in order to properly balance factors such as quantities of cannabinoids and THC (the main chemicals in marijuana), cold or disease resistance, or speed of flowering cycles. In the beginning, there were only a handful of marijuana strains found naturally outdoors.

But because of cross-pollination and other techniques, creating hybrids has become far easier to combine the best qualities of each individual type of weed into one ideal set of strains.

One can also find different flavors of hybrids; some have a sweeter pineapple or strawberry taste while others are said to resemble the tangy citrus of oranges.

It is really a matter of finding the type that you enjoy best and benefit the most out of. Luckily, you have many options to choose from!

WHAT ARE THC AND CBD?

Throughout this book so far, you may be wondering what THC and CBD actually are– that is, if you are unfamiliar with marijuana, its effects, and its chemistry. It is a pretty quick and simple explanation, so keep on reading.

THC

Weed 101: THC is short for tetrahydrocannabinol, and it is what makes one feel either relaxed, creative, or any other reaction that affects one's perception of their five senses after consuming a strain.

There are bits of evidence to support that a high amount of THC aids the body in relieving pain and improving one's overall condition. As a result, that's why people with certain chronic illnesses or ailments of any sort prefer strains with more of this chemical for its medicinal purposes.

CBD

As a whole, CBD goes hand in hand with THC. It can weaken or strengthen specific characteristics of THC, making it a more viable option for individuals who may not want to affect their senses so much as to relieve pain or improve their sleeping patterns, anxiety, or eating habits.

Essentially, people who only want the medicinal qualities of marijuana without the psychoactive effects seek out strains with a greater ratio of CBD than THC.

EXTRACTING AND STORING THC

Now, what is always worthwhile to know is how to properly extract and store THC for personalized usage. The basic rule to follow is: the higher the quality preferred, the drier the cannabis must be.

With the exception of extract from the resinous sections, the whole plant may be utilized for extraction through some sort of solvent, such as alcohol. In the next few sections, we will talk more about how to use solvents and solventless methods, along with how to make other types of extractions.

If you are already aware of how to do all of this, or you would rather purchase cannabis-infused butter or oil instead of making your own, feel free to skip away until you find a more entertaining chapter.

EXTRACTION METHODS

Let's break this down into solventless and solvent-based extraction methods. The first category involves water (solventless method), while the second one covers alcohol, propane, or butane, among others (solvent-based method). Do take in mind that using propane or butane is a far less recommended option than alcohol.

Now, aside from extracting THC for the psychoactive shenanigans, one can also do the same for CBD in order to get the medicinal aspect of cannabis, as we reviewed earlier.

SOLVENTLESS CANNABIS EXTRACTS

Once we truly get the basics in our mind, we can go onto the actual steps to follow and the various kinds of cannabis extracts we can make. The question here would be, how?

Some might assume all of the parts in this process will be complicated and ridden with unnecessarily expensive equipment. Instead of being discouraged by an assumption, fear not. Take a deep breath, unclench your wallet from that nervous grip, and keep on reading.

The answer may be found in the number four. Four seasons, four elements, four pieces used to make cannabis extracts. Water, a sieve, pressure, and heat.

HASH

First, quick terminology prologue (bear with me for a second). Trichomes are microscopically-tiny stems with a transparent bulb at the top; they are found all throughout the surface of marijuana plants. Now, this is relevant because trichomes contain the oils we wish to extract for our hash.

Bubble hash, otherwise known as ice water cannabis concentrate, will require a mason jar or glass bowl, several cups of chipped ice, water, a large, clean bucket, a couple of spoons, a wooden spatula, and two large cheesecloths.

The first step is to fill a Mason jar or bowl with your cannabis and freeze it overnight, as the brittleness will be helpful later on. The next day, lay out your cheesecloth around the edges of the bucket while letting the remaining fabric loosely cover the inside nook. Repeat this process with the second cheesecloth.

Once your bucket is set up with the cheesecloths, place your frozen cannabis in it along with three to four cups of chipped ice. Pour three cups of water in the center of the ice, and use the spatula to stir with plenty of elbow grease until the ice is completely melted.

When all the liquid is gone from the first cheesecloth, remove it and dispose of the now-damp cannabis however you see fit. Stir the remaining liquid in the second cheesecloth until it has all gone through the bucket.

Now, this is where it gets a bit more intense. After the second cheesecloth is removed and all the water is at the bottom of the bucket, stretch the cloth and very thoroughly scrape off the foam accumulated at the surface with the spoon until you reach a small clump of a substance resembling light brown wet clay.

Dip only a small portion of the cheesecloth on the foaming surface of the cannabis water you extracted, and keep repeating the process of scraping at the foam and the clumps.

The resulting bubble hash should be pressed against two clean towels as to remove any excess moisture, and they are now good to go.

Another vocabulary word to take into
consideration is kief. These are compiled crystals
gathered from the leaves, buds, and stems from a
cannabis plant. Sounds familiar? That is because it is
very much so: Kief is also another word for trichomes.

Instead of using a lengthy process with water and ice, kief may be extracted using a three-chamber grinder bought at a legal cannabis dispensary.

ROSIN

Imagine a golden, translucent, bubble-ridden substance that is very prone to shattering. Liquid gold in the world of cannabis, really, rosin is the resulting sap from adding pressurized heat to the ice water cannabis concentrate or the flower buds directly.

The way to make it is the in-between something as simple as a grinder for kief and the more complicated process of extracting hash. The tools you will need are narrowed down to heat-resistant gloves, parchment or waxed paper, a hair straightener, and a spoon.

For the actual method of extraction, it is recommended to watch a few tutorials online, asking a worker at your local dispensary, or reading a few articles.

Even though the research could be omitted and one could just dive right into guessing how to make rosin, it may result in a potential loss of money and a few eyebrow hairs if one does not take the necessary precautions.

Remember: protect your eyebrows, do not be wasteful with your purchases, and make it a point to keep yourself well-informed.

SOLVENT-BASED CANNABIS EXTRACTS

BUTANE HASH OIL (BHO)

Just as a friendly health-conscious reminder, butane is typically used for lighter fluid; it is highly flammable and prone to explode if it is not handled properly with the right equipment.

With that said, this is technically a staple when it comes to solvents used for THC extractions. BHO as a whole can branch off into nectar, wax, or oil, to name a few– the names depend on the texture of the final product. This is a pretty standard way of recognizing the various types of byproducts available.

Rick Simpson Oil (RSO)

Rick Simpson is one of the main advocates for the use of medicinal marijuana. He was diagnosed with skin cancer back in 2002, and after the regular set of treatments did not improve his condition, Simpson opted to try medicinal marijuana ointments and oils. Within days, the cancerous bumps on his arms disappeared. After a few more weeks, his cancer was completely eradicated.

As a heavy believer in the astounding properties of cannabis, Rick Simpson decided to produce his own oil and make it available–free of charge–to the masses. He also provided the recipe for the one he made that healed his cancer.

If you wish to make it in your home, the recipe for Rick Simpson Oil, also called Phoenix Tears, may be found at his website.

Supercritical Fluid Extraction (CO2)

This is the part where the methods get a bit more eccentric. There are a few odd ways to extract things, some including dry ice or liquid nitrogen, but in this case, a company would be using carbon dioxide to extract hash oil.

The science behind this method involves using carbon dioxide– the solvent– to separate the oil from the plant matter in an extremely clean, safe way. In order for industries and companies to fulfill this process, the carbon dioxide must be in supercritical fluid form; in other words, it varies back and forth in all the three states of matter.

Quick pro-tip: it is not recommended to employ this method without the proper equipment, which typically is rather expensive. So, if possible, opt for a more rustic fashion of extracting your cannabis oils.

MOLECULAR SEPARATION

Another method utilized for industrial purposes of cannabis oil production: molecular separation. That's right. We have heard about carbon dioxide and ice water, but now we are hitting the tip of the proverbial iceberg with a molecular level of precision.

While the name 'molecular separation' may appear slightly intimidating, it really just is a distillation method with alarmingly specific temperatures and equipment in order to not damage the plant too much with the heat source in case. That last concept is called thermal degradation, for future references.

TINCTURES

Tinctures are made through alcohol extraction— or using alcohol as a solvent to acquire the desired cannabinoids for your personal use. Now, there is evidence to support that it is safer to use ethanol as opposed to isopropyl alcohol because the latter contains more toxins.

The first preparation one should do drying and freezing their cannabis flowers, leaves, or stems (also remember to freeze the alcohol you intend to use). Afterward, pour alcohol over the jar of frozen cannabis, and place the jar in the freezer and stir the mixture at intervals of two to five minutes at a time.

Eventually, the alcohol must be purged from the tincture through a vacuum and a safe heat source, so it is not exactly a method one should use at home without any prior knowledge and a fire extinguisher.

There are also alternative methods incorporating low-proof vodka instead of isopropyl or ethanol, which eliminates the purging part of the equation.

Regardless, it is always, always best to speak to your local dispensary employees or someone with more experience on the field; do your research, and take thorough notes, so you do not waste money, cannabis, or other resources.

LIVE RESIN

So, this technique depends entirely on how fresh the cannabis is, and how immediately it was frozen after its harvest. The general rule of thumb is to not use dry portions of the plant, but rather keep it as fresh as humanly possible.

You will then have 36 hours to pour a solvent through it, keeping the temperatures very cold throughout this time (as the solvent should also be previously chilled).

In a way, this is one of the faster methods, as the others require about 70 days of curing and preparing your cannabis before running any type of extraction for it.

DECARBOXYLATION METHOD

In order to activate the psychoactive properties of marijuana, one must either dry and age the plant or heat it. Even though the first method does work, it does not always preserve a large portion of the chemicals that allow one to get either the high or the medicinal characteristics of cannabis. That's where decarboxylation comes in.

Decarboxylation– also known as activating or decarbing – is the process that employs heat to change the cannabinoids in the plant into a form the body can process. Want to know more about this method? Look down below.

WHY DECARB?

Now, you might ask me, why do we need to go through this seemingly long and unnecessary process, oh author? Quite simple, really. Decarbing before cooking will help in making the most out of your cannabis purchase, regardless of the reason one got it in the first place (we do not judge in this book, as long as there are no lawsuits for hypothetical cases).

So, it is the opposite of an unnecessary process, since skipping it would lessen your cannabinoids' potency by more than half percent.

HOW TO DECARB CANNABIS

How should you use the decarboxylation method on your own, without fire extinguishers or expensive equipment? You will need a baking sheet, an oven, a food processor, and a wooden or heatproof spatula.

1. Your oven must be preheated to 240°F.
2. Separate and tear one ounce (for starters, but use more if your edibles recipe calls for it) of your cannabis into smaller pieces.
3. Place a thin, even layer of your plant on the surface of a baking sheet lined with wax paper and bake it for 30 to 40 minutes while stirring every 10 minutes.
4. Once your marijuana bits are closer to golden brown in color, remove it from the oven (very carefully) and lay it out to cool.

After it is cool to the touch, place your toasted cannabis into a food processor and use the pulse setting until it is coarsely ground. Store in a proper container somewhere cool until you are ready to use it.

How to Calculate a THC Dosage for Recipes

Generally-speaking, cannabis contains about 10-12% THC on average. We will look at a bit of math and equivalencies for a moment here:

- An eighth of cannabis = 3.5 grams
- A quarter ounce = 7 grams
- A gram of cannabis = 1,000 milligrams
- Example: let's pretend you have an average strain weighing 1,000 milligrams, containing 10% THC. You want that percentage into milligrams, so 10% of 1,000mg converts into 100mg (all you need to do is divide 1,000 by 10), giving you a total of 100mg of THC in that strain you can work with for your recipes.

In order to find out approximately how much cannabis is in each serving of your recipe, allow me to illustrate some slightly rough contextual math:

- If you have at your disposal 4g of your plant equaling 400mg of THC, all you need to do is divide that number (400mg) by the number of servings in your recipe. Consequently, 50 chocolate chip cookies would give you 8mg of THC per cookie.

Quick recommendation: 5mg of THC per serving is said to be the ideal dose for people who have not previously dived into the world of edibles and cannabis consumption and are now dipping their toe into the proverbial pool.

It is always best to take it easy and consume small doses while building your tolerance in the long-term.

TIPS FOR COOKING WITH CANNABIS

As with anything, there are certain procedures, precautions, and rules to follow when it comes to cooking, and that will not change by adding cannabis to a recipe. After all, caramel will still burn you if it gets on your skin, and something will catch on fire if there are napkins or towels next to an open flame. Common sense, people. It cannot be stressed enough times that common sense in a kitchen is an extremely important tool.

Keep yourself and your work area clean, pull back your long hair (if that applies to you, because we all know finding hair in your food is similar to a Lovecraftian tale of horror), do not leave any heat sources unattended, and use a designated set for your cannabis-infused desserts so the other bits of kitchen equipment is not contaminated.

As for the actual consumption of your desserts, remember the following:

1. Wait for an hour or two after eating your edibles, as they take a while to kick in. The effects are definitely not as instant as when cannabis is smoked, so be patient, and avoid eating several all at once, since that is linked to pretty nightmarish situations.
2. Backing up your edibles with fatty-based, protein-packed foods like milk might lengthen the effects of THC.

3. Marijuana has a very specific scent. Some think it is earthy; others believe it smells like burning trash– regardless of what it reminds people of, we can all agree it is pretty distinguishable. As you cook, ventilate your kitchen, so your clothes or items do not wind up smelling like a local dispensary.

4. In the case of accidentally getting too high, bluntly-speaking, the main liquids you can eat and activities to do consist of: drinking water or juice (NOT caffeinated drinks), eat salty snacks, do a relaxing activity like watching a show you enjoy or drawing. Essentially, hydrate yourself and find a way to pass the time while the effects subside.

With that in mind, it's time to make cannabutter!

ESSENTIAL INGREDIENTS FOR COOKING WITH CANNABIS

THC and CBD bind with ingredients that are fatty in nature. That is why cream, oil, butter, coconut butter, and milk are typically used for infusions and edibles. There are other ways, though, so we will look at a few to make cannabutter, cannaoil, cannaflour, canna-syrup, and cannabis coconut butter.

CANNABIS BUTTER (CANNABUTTER)

Equipment needed:

- Large Saucepan
- Wooden Spatula
- Spoon
- Fine Sieve
- Heat-Proof Lidded Container

Ingredients:

- 1/2 ounce finely ground cannabis buds
- 1 cup (two sticks) of unsalted butter left at room temperature to soften.

Procedure:

1. Place both sticks of butter in the saucepan after heating it up in a low flame for a few seconds. Maintain that temperature until all the butter is completely melted, making sure it does not burn.

2. Slowly spoon small quantities of your ground cannabis into the melted butter, and stir until it is all incorporated together. Have it stew altogether during 45-50 minutes, stirring periodically.

   *This is where ventilating your kitchen and reading a good book or watching a movie (or even getting some work done) would come in pretty handy while you wait and stir.

3. Once there are bubbles at the surface of your mixture, remove your pan from the heat.

4. Use the spoon and the sieve to help you strain your cannabutter (very carefully) into the designated heat-proof container, leave out to cool completely, then place the lid on top and refrigerate or use as soon as you wish to.

Cannabis Cream

Equipment needed:

- Fine Metal Sieve

- Double Boiler

- Heat-Proof Lidded Container

- Wooden or Heat-Proof Silicone Spatula

Ingredients:

- 7 grams of finely-ground cannabis

- 1 cup of heavy whipping cream

Procedure:

1. Heat the whipping cream on your double boiler until there is fine steam on its surface and bits of foam form on the sides of the saucepan.

2. Bit by bit, incorporate the dried, ground cannabis into the cream. Stir momentarily, then

keep the flame at a low heat, allowing the mixture to steep for a minimum of two hours. Remember to stir every ten minutes so the heavy cream does not stick and burn to the bottom of the saucepan.

3. After the two hours, turn off your stove and wait for the temperature of the cream to drop, so it is lukewarm rather than boiling hot.

4. Once it hits that point, strain it with the fine sieve until there are no bits of the actual plant left floating around, and pour your mixture into the heat-proof container. Refrigerate until you intend to use it, and enjoy.

   Fun fact: this infusion will still make for very fluffy whipping cream, so do not worry about the consistency. The key point with heavy cream as a whole is not to overbeat it, otherwise, it will start to turn into butter.

CANNABIS OIL (CANNA OIL)

Equipment needed:

- Fine Sieve

- Crock-pot/Slow Cooker
- Wooden Spatula
- Heat-proof Lidded Container
- Spoon

Ingredients:

- 1 cup of finely ground marijuana

- 1 cup of vegetable oil

Procedure:

1. 1. Incorporate your ground plant into the vegetable oil using the crock-pot. Place it on a low temperature for around five hours, checking and stirring it all through every so often to make sure it is cooking evenly.

   *The mixture should always stay at a temperature below 240 degrees Fahrenheit.

2. If there is occasional fear of burning, add a quarter cup of water every two hours.

3. After watching the director's cut of a single Lord of the Rings film– or after five hours– your oil should be good to go. Turn off the crock-pot, strain the cannaoil, and place in the refrigerator for four months, at most.

CANNABIS COCONUT OIL

On average, coconut oil has a tendency to absorb cannabis at a greater rate compared to regular vegetable oil or butter. There are more complex steps, so bear with me for a moment, as this is a worthwhile procedure used to make the most out of your recipes.

Equipment:

- Crock-pot

- Fine Sieve

- Food Thermometer

Ingredients:

- ½ cup of coconut oil

- ½ tsp. sunflower lecithin

- ½ cup of finely ground, dry cannabis

- ¼ cup of Water

Procedure:

1. The coconut oil, water, and sunflower lecithin are mixed inside the crock-pot, which is then set at a high temperature.
2. Slowly sprinkle the dried marijuana into the mixture, adding water as one deems necessary. Close the crock-pot lid and use the thermometer to check the temperature every five minutes– ensuring the thermometer never touches the sides or bottom of the saucepan.
3. Once the oil reaches 245°F, switch over to a low heat mode and maintain a steady temperature, ensuring the mixture never surpasses 320°F. Allow it to cook for two and a half hours, stirring every 10 minutes.
4. The oil must be cool to the touch but still warm

enough for the coconut portion of it to remain liquid. Strain your cannabis-infused coconut oil with the aid of a spoon or spatula (anything that can help you push the plant matter into the strain and extract as much of the oil as possible) right into a mason jar or a container with an airtight lid.

5. Keep your oil in the refrigerator or use immediately, depending on your personal needs.

CANNABIS FLOUR

Acquire dry cannabis buds, or alternatively, purchase regular cannabis and dry and decarboxylate it through any of the previous methods we mentioned earlier in this book. As long as there is absolutely no moisture in your plant, your flour is foolproof. It is a very simple process involving grinding the buds, digging around for any whole bits, grind those, and keep repeating and grinding in a food processor until you have an extremely fine powder or flour.

This should be stored in an airtight container and used within a day, or kept in a refrigerator and incorporated into recipes when the occasion calls for it.

CANNABIS CORN SYRUP

Equipment:

- Crock-Pot

- Extra Fine Metal Sieve

- Spoon or Heat-Proof Spatula

- Heat-Proof Glass Container

Ingredients:

- 2 Cups of Light Corn Syrup
- 1 Cup of Finely-Ground Cannabis
- 1 Tablespoon of Butter
- Water

Procedure:

1. Mix in the syrup, water, and butter in the crock-pot at a medium heat mode. Pour your dried, ground cannabis in a slow and steady fashion (as we have done so many times before by this point, you are already a master on the subject) into the heated syrup mixture.
2. Steep your syrup for 3 hours, stirring frequently, and adding water as needed for the mixture not to burn.
3. You know what's coming next– cool the syrup down until it can be handled safely, strain it, store it, and keep it refrigerated. See how simple this turned out?

Now that we officially have all of the terms, chemistry notes, and extraction methods out of the way, we can put everything we have learned to the test with these incoming international recipes.

Whatever suits your fancy, if you enjoy all things sweet, you will be satisfied with any of the desserts listed below.

RECIPES

FRENCH CARIBBEAN FLAMED CANNABUTTER BANANAS

Equipment:

- One Stainless Steel Saucepan
- Wooden Spatula
- Measuring Cup
- Measuring Spoon
- Knife

Ingredients:

- 2 tablespoons of Cannabutter
- 3 tablespoons of granulated sugar
- Two Same-Sized Bananas
- ¼ cup of Rum
- Vanilla Ice Cream

Procedure:

1. Gently melt the cannabutter on the frying pan at a low heat, until it is completely liquid.

2. Add the sugar, stir with the wooden spatula, and wait as the sugar dissolves into the butter and begins to bubble.

3. Once it reaches a thicker texture and a golden brown color, cut the bananas vertically from top to bottom, so you have two halves of one banana, or four halves after cutting the second one. Carefully place your bananas, flat-side down, into the caramel sauce.

4. Spoon the sauce onto the uncovered parts of your bananas.

5. This is where it gets a bit flammable. Remove the pan from the heat, and with utmost care, tip the pan sideways, so all the sauce is pooled together on one part without dripping onto your stove. At a safe distance, add the rum, tip your pan back onto its regular position, and watch as the delicate (but still very, very much hot) flames caramelize the bananas. *The flames are a result of the alcohol evaporating when it comes in contact with the heat of the sugar and cannabutter.

6. After the flames dissipate completely, plate your dish with plenty of sauce in the dish. Add a scoop of vanilla ice cream on top of the bananas. Enjoy!

CANNABIS CARAMELS

Ingredients:

- 1 cup <u>cannabutter</u>
- ½ of a cup brown sugar
- A pinch of salt
- 1 cup light corn syrup
- 1 can of sweetened condensed milk

Instructions:

1. Melt the butter before adding brown sugar and salt.

2. Stir until combined.

3. Add light corn syrup to the mix. Gradually add milk while stirring constantly.

4. Cook and stir over medium heat, until the candy reaches a firm ball stage, which should take about 12 to 15 minutes.

5. Remove the mix from heat; Add vanilla and pour into a 9" by 13" pan.

6. Let it cool, cut in square shape and wrap.

High Ranchers

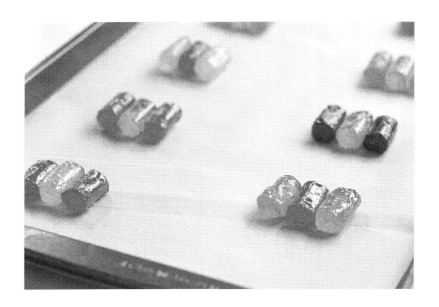

Ingredients:

- 2 cups of raw sugar

- Cannabis corn syrup (2/3 cup)

- Add your choice of flavoring. Usually, you need only a few drops of extract for making candy

- Food coloring (1-2 drops)

-

Instructions:

- Mix the sugar, flavoring, color, and syrup until they are mixed together.
- Heat until your liquid is 295 F.
- Remove the mix from the oven and add your flavoring.
- Line trays with wax paper and place in the freezer for one hour.
- Cut into pieces.

Equipment:

- A 6-inch pie tin
- Medium-Sized Whisk
- Medium-Sized Bowl
- Heat-Proof Spatula
- Medium Saucepan

Ingredients:

For the pastry-

- ¾ cup of all-purpose flour

- 3 tablespoons of granulated sugar

- A pinch of salt

- 4 tablespoons of cold cannabutter

- 1 egg yolk

- Uncooked beans

For the filling-

- 1 ⅛ cups of milk

- 1 tablespoon of softened cannabutter

- ¼ teaspoon of nutmeg

- ½ teaspoon of powdered cinnamon

- 1 tablespoon of all-purpose flour

- 1 tablespoon of cornstarch

- ¼ cup of granulated sugar

- Half of a vanilla bean, seeds scraped off and placed in a bowl, or 1 teaspoon of vanilla extract
- 1 large organic egg
- Cinnamon to sprinkle

Procedure:

1. Preheat oven to 375° Fahrenheit.
2. In a bowl, sift the flour and combine with the salt and sugar.
3. Add the frozen cannabutter in cubes or smaller pieces that will make for a crumbly dough after some heavy-duty stirring, then incorporate the egg yolk.
4. This is the part where you begin to knead it on a flat, clean surface until it is all combined.
5. Use a bit more of cannabutter (or regular butter) to grease the entire pie pan, then gently press your dough onto the bottom and the sides of the pan, so it is completely covered.
6. Pour two handfuls of uncooked beans into the pan (allows the dough to remain flat against the tin) and bake the dough for 15-20 minutes, or

until it has a golden brown color. Leave it out to cool.

7. In the medium saucepan, mix in and heat the cannabutter, the milk, the cinnamon, and the nutmeg at low heat. Stir until the butter is fully mixed in with the milk. Leave the saucepan off the heat momentarily.

8. Whisk together the sugar, flour, cornstarch, and egg for your pie filling in a separate mixing bowl.

9. Scoop two spoonfuls of the warm milk and cannabutter mixture and stir them quickly into the bowl with the egg*. Add another spoonful along with the vanilla paste/extract, stir, then pour the contents of the bowl into the saucepan with the rest of the milk. Place it all on the stove at a medium-heat flame and whisk nonstop as the custard reaches a smooth, pudding-like texture.

   a. *This is to prevent your eggs from cooking aggressively and turning into a scrambled mess instead of a homogenous custard cream.

10.   After 5 minutes, it should be evenly cooked, and   we can pour it into the pie pan. Sprinkle it with cinnamon powder, wait until it cools down a bit, and freeze it until you are ready to eat a delicious milk tart.

MARIJUANA GUMMY BEARS

Ingredients:

- Cannabis oil – 2 Oz.

- Large box of jelly cubes of any flavor

- 6 packets of unflavored gelatin

- ½ cup of cold water

- Gummy molds

- Various food coloring

Instructions:

1. Mix all of the jelly cubes, coloring, packets of gelatin and water in a small saucepan.

2. Mix the ingredients until they reach a dough-like consistency.

3. Place the saucepan on medium heat, and continue to stir until the mixture melts back into a liquid consistency.

4. Add in cannabis oil and mix.

5. Pour the mixture into a jug.

6. Pour the mixture into the candy molds.

7. Place the molds in the freezer for 15-20 minutes; this will set the cannabis gummy bears ready to be removed from the molds.

8. Take the mold out from the freezer, and carefully remove the gummy bears.

- To make them in different colors, mix each color separately, pour each color in a different mold.

Equipment:

- Two Large Mixing Bowls
- Plastic Wrapper
- Two large baking trays
- Whisk
- Heatproof Silicone Spatula

- One Fork
- Measuring Cups
- Measuring Spoons
- Pyrex Measuring Glass

Ingredients:

- 1 organic egg yolk

- ½ cup of butter (¼ cup of regular unsalted butter and ¼ cup of cannabutter)

- 1 cup of all-purpose flour

- ½ cup of almond flour

- ⅓ cup of sugar

- ½ teaspoon of baking soda

- ¼ teaspoon of salt

- A bag of whole almonds

Procedure:

1. Sift your two types of flour together, and add the baking soda and salt in the first bowl.
2. In the second bowl, mix your butter (cannabis-infused and regular), sugar, and egg yolk until there are no random streaks of darker orange.
3. Whisk your dry ingredients into the wet ones and stir everything together. By this point, you should have a very doughy type of texture, which you will further knead on a clean, flat surface. All the flour should be completely combined through, and the resulting ball of dough should be relatively moist and malleable. Wrap it in plastic and place it in the fridge for at least one hour.
4. Preheat the oven to 165° Fahrenheit. Scoop small golf ball-sized portions of the dough, shape into spheres, and gently press the fork into a criss-cross pattern (first vertical press, then horizontal).
5. Carefully push the almond into the center of the dough ball. Repeat until all the dough is shaped and decorated with an almond.

6. Place the balls on the baking tray making sure to leave enough space between each. Let them bake for 20 minutes, turn off the oven, and keep the cookies there for approximately 7 minutes before getting them out. They should be warm, soft at first then crunchy, and with a very characteristic almond taste. Happy munching.

GANJA POPSICLES

Ingredients:

- 2 mangos, peeled and chopped into small chunks

- 2 cups vanilla yogurt

- 4 tablespoons of coconut cream

- 2-3 tablespoons of cannabis coconut oil

- 3 tablespoons of coconut sugar

- 2 teaspoons of coconut extract

Instructions:

1. Place all of the ingredients into a blender until they are smooth.

2. Pour them into Popsicle molds.

3. Freeze and enjoy!

CANNABIS CUPCAKES

Ingredients:

- 1 box of cake mix

- ¼ cup of water

- 1/3 cup of cannabis oil or cannabutter or ½ ounce of ground cannabis

- 3 eggs

- 1 cup chocolate chips

- 1 container of frosting

- 2 packets cupcake liners

- 2 grams of cannabis kief

Instructions:

1. Pre-heat the oven to 325 degrees.

2. Empty the whole box of cake mix into a large sized bowl.

3. Add the eggs, the cannabis oil, and the water.

4. Beat at low speed for 30 seconds. Then continue beating at medium speed for 2 minutes.

5. Add the chocolate chips and beat until creamy.

6. Line the cupcake tray with the cupcake liners and fill each cupcake liner with the mix, leaving space for the mix to rise.

Add a little cannabis kief on top of each mix and stir to mix the kief in.

7. Place the lined tray in the oven and heat for it for 15 to 20 minutes.

8. Remove the tray. Leave it to cool for 20-25 minutes.

9. Frost the cupcakes.

Cannabis Chocolate Chip Cookies

Ingredients:

- ¾ cup cannabis butter

- 2 large eggs

- 1 cup brown sugar

- ½ Cup white sugar

- 1 Tablespoon vanilla extract

- 2¼ cups all-purpose flour

- ¾ teaspoon baking soda

- ½ teaspoon fine salt

- 1 bag of chocolate chips

Instructions:

1. Preheat the oven to 375 F and grease two cookie sheets with regular butter, or line them with parchment paper.

2. First, melt the cannabutter in a small saucepan then allow it to cool slightly.

3. Place the eggs, sugars, and vanilla in a large bowl, add the melted butter and whisk the contents together.

4. In a medium bowl, mix the flour, baking soda, and salt. Once the dry ingredients are incorporated, slowly stir the first bowl of the wet ingredients in with the dry.

5. Pour in the chocolate chips.

6. Scoop out about ¼ cup of cookie dough for each cookie and drop onto the prepared pans. Leave enough space between each cookie for them to grow.

7. Bake cookies for 12 to 16 minutes.

8. Store in a sealed container up to 4 days.

No-Bake Chocolate Marijuana Cookies

Ingredients:

- 1 ½ cups quick-cooking oats
- ½ cup flaked coconut

- ¼ cup chopped walnuts
- ¾ cup sugar
- ¼ cup milk
- ¼ cup (half stick) cannabis butter
- 1 cup creamy peanut butter
- 3 tbsp. Unsweetened cocoa

Instructions:

1. In a medium bowl combine oats, coconut, and walnuts; set aside.

2. In a medium saucepan combine sugar, milk, cannabis butter, and cocoa. Cook over medium heat, stirring occasionally, and bring to a boil.

3. Remove from heat. Stir in the oats mixture and peanut butter.

4. Quickly drop mixture onto waxed paper, using a teaspoon.

5. Let it cool completely. Store in an airtight container in the refrigerator.

Cannabis Peanut Butter Balls

Ingredients:

- 1 cup oatmeal
- ½ cup peanut butter, creamy or chunky
- ¼ cup sweetened dried coconut
- 3 tablespoons cocoa
- 1 teaspoon instant espresso
- 1 teaspoon vanilla
- 3 tablespoons cannabutter, softened

- 3 tablespoons honey
- 3 tablespoons powdered sugar
- 2 tablespoons cocoa

Instructions:

1. In a medium bowl mix all the ingredients except the powdered sugar and remaining cocoa powder.

2. Stir to blend well and chill for 35 minutes.

3. In another bowl combine the powdered sugar and the cocoa.

4. Divide the chilled mixture into 12 portions, form each into a ball by hand and roll each on the sugar/cocoa mix. Place them on a sheet of parchment or waxed paper as you go.

5. Store in refrigerator or freezer until ready to use.

MARIJUANA FUDGE

Ingredients:

- 454 grams of cannabis butter

- 1.6 kilos of powdered sugar

- 240 grams cocoa powder

- 1 tsp vanilla extract

- 240 grams of peanut butter

Instructions:

1. Melt the cannabis butter and peanut butter together on the stove in a double boiler.

2. Add the flavors of your choosing.

3. Mix the dry ingredients separately.

4. Remove the double boiler from the heat and combine wet and dry in a bowl. Mix thoroughly.

5. When properly mixed, transfer contents into your fudge or baking pan

6. Press down into shape. Place in a chilled environment.

Marijuana Red Velvet Brownies

Ingredients for the base:

- 3 ½ oz. milk chocolate
- ¾ cup cannabutter
- 3 large organic eggs
- 1 cup sugar
- 1 teaspoon vanilla powder
- 2 tablespoons red food coloring
- 1 cup of barley flour

- 2 tablespoons cocoa powder
- ¼ teaspoon sea salt

Ingredients for the cheesecake frosting:

- 8 ounces cream cheese, room temperature
- ¼ cup organic granulated sugar
- 1 large organic egg, lightly beaten
- 1/2 teaspoon vanilla powder
- ¼ teaspoon sea salt
- 1 tablespoon barley flour

Instructions:

1. Preheat the oven to 350F. Grease an 8x10 pan with cooking spray. Put up the chocolate in a heatproof bowl with the butter. Set the bowl over a saucepan of steaming hot water and melt gently, stirring frequently. Remove the bowl from the saucepan and leave to cool until needed.

2. Break the eggs into a mixing bowl and beat well with a whisk or an electric mixer. Add the sugar and the vanilla and whisk until the mixture is very thick and mousse-like - about 4 minutes.

3. Whisk in the melted chocolate mixture and the food coloring. Sift the flour, cocoa, and salt into the mixture and mix until thoroughly combined. Transfer the mixture to the prepared pan and spread evenly.

4. To make the frosting, combine the cream cheese and sugar in a bowl and whip with an electric mixer. Add vanilla powder and egg to combine. By hand, slowly mix in the flour and salt. Stir until combined. Drop the mix of the mixture, evenly spaced, onto the chocolate mix.

5. Bake the mix in a preheated oven for about 20-25 minutes. The final result should be slightly fudgy with crumbs attached.

CANNABIS CORN SYRUP ANZAC COOKIES

Equipment:

- Mixing Bowl
- Wooden Spatula
- Medium Saucepan
- Large Baking Tray
- Whisk

Ingredients:

- ½ cup of oats

- ½ cup of flour

- ½ cup of sugar

- ½ cup of shredded coconut

- 1 tablespoon of cannabis corn syrup

- 1 teaspoon of water

- 4 tablespoons of butter

- ½ teaspoon of baking soda

Procedure:

1. In the bowl, combine your dry ingredients: sifted flour, sugar, oats, and shredded coconut. Once you are done with that, preheat the oven to 370° Fahrenheit and grease your baking tray with some cannabutter.

2. Using low heat and a saucepan, melt the butter. Pour in your water and cannabis corn syrup (as seen in the procedures we mentioned earlier in this book).

3. Stir with the spatula until everything is well-incorporated, then add baking soda after turning off the stove and removing the pan from the heat.

4. Bit by bit, stir in the butter-water-syrup mix into the flour and oats until you have a workable dough and there are no streaks of white from unstirred dry components.

5. Shape walnut-sized chunks of dough into spheres and place them on top of the prepared tray, leaving a 2-inch space all-around between each cookie (they spread a lot as they bake).

6. Bake the cookies for 10-15 minutes, depending on the texture you would like them to have.

New England Cheddar-Apple Ganja Cookies

Equipment:

- Two large mixing bowls
- Whisk
- Measuring Spoons
- Dry Measuring Cups
- Baking Cookie Sheet

Ingredients:

- ¾ cups of All-Purpose Flour
- ¼ cup of Baking Soda

- ¼ cup of Powdered Cinnamon
- ¼ cup of Salt
- 2 tablespoons of Light Brown Sugar
- 2 tablespoons of Granulated Sugar
- ¼ cup of Cannabutter
- 1 Egg
- ½ teaspoon of Vanilla
- 6 tablespoons Shredded Sharp Cheddar Cheese
- ¾ cups of Chopped and Peeled Granny Smith Apples
- 4 tablespoons of Pecans

Instructions:

1. Preheat your oven to 370° Fahrenheit.

2. Sift the flour and whisk in the baking soda, cinnamon, and salt so that you have one bowl of dry ingredients.

3. Make sure your cannabutter is set at room temperature before you cream it along with the sugar, egg, and vanilla.

4. Combine the wet ingredients into the dry ones, including your chopped apples, pecans, and shreds of Cheddar.

5. Use a tablespoon and your hands to shape the cookie dough into spheres, which we will place into a baking tray lined with non-stick paper. If you want, you could even add a few more bits of Cheddar to the top of the spheres so they have a crispy cheesy surface.

6. Bake for 20 minutes, or until you get that very characteristic warm, sugared apple scent wafting all around your kitchen.

POT DE CRÈME AU CHOCOLAT

Equipment:

- Four 5 oz. Ramekins

- Whisk

- Fine Sieve

- Two Large Mixing Bowls

- Medium-Sized Saucepan

- Glass Baking Dish

- Measuring Spoons

- Dry and Liquid Measuring Cups

- Aluminum Foil

Ingredients:

- ½ cup of Chopped Dark Chocolate
- ¼ cup of Chopped Milk Chocolate
- ¾ cup of Heavy Cream
- ¼ cup of Cannabis-Infused Heavy Cream
- 3 Large, Organic Egg Yolks
- 1 teaspoon of vanilla extract or vanilla scraped from the pod
- ¼ teaspoon of salt

Procedure:

1. Preheat oven to 320° Fahrenheit.

2. Pour both your regular and cannabis-infused heavy creams into the saucepan and bring them close to a boil (you will see steam rising and frothy bubbles forming along the sides of where the cream touches the pan). Place your chocolate pieces inside the mixing bowl while you wait.

3. Remove the cream from the heat, pour it in the same bowl as your chocolate, and leave the mixture alone for two minutes. After that point, stir your ganache (melted chocolate and cream sauce) until it is smooth.

4. In the meantime, beat the egg yolks and the sugar together. The resulting mixture should have a light, pastel yellow color and have a fluffy texture. At that point, toss in the vanilla extract or vanilla paste and the salt.

5. Stir in two spoonfuls of your chocolate sauce to the yolk mixture, then once it is all incorporated, add the remainder of it.

6. With the help of a regular metal spoon and your sieve, strain the resulting custard, making sure every lump is carefully disintegrated.

7. Once the chocolate custard is strained and looks smooth, it practically reflects any surface (hyperbole), divide the mixture into the four ramekins, and position those in the glass baking dish. Fill the dish with water until it covers the ramekins halfway, and cover everything with foil. *Pro-tip: it is far, far easier to pour water into the baking dish once it is already positioned inside the oven. We want to avoid juggling desserts as much as possible.

8. Bake the custards for 35 minutes. It might be difficult to tell, but the surface should be set in the center while jiggling slightly along the sides of the ramekin. The toothpick trick will not work here, unfortunately.

9. After 35 minutes, VERY carefully remove the individual ramekins from the baking dish (remember: no juggling with boiling water either), wait for them to cool, then freeze them

overnight. They are good to go by that point and may be decorated with anything from salted caramel to whipped cannabis-infused cream.

Buddy Brazilian Brigadeiros

Equipment:

- Medium Saucepan
- Wooden Spatula
- Medium Mixing Bowl

Ingredients:

- 1 Can of Sweetened Condensed Milk
- 1 tablespoon of Cannabutter

- 3 tablespoons of Unsweetened Cocoa Powder
- Dark Chocolate Sprinkles

Procedure:

1. Toss the condensed milk, cannabutter, and cocoa powder inside the saucepan and warm them at medium heat.

2. Stir them together until they are fully incorporated into a thick cream fudge, which should take about 10-15 minutes*.

*Pro-Tip: If you tilt the saucepan and the mixture does not stick to the bottom, the dessert has the texture we are looking for.

3. Grease a bowl with a bit more cannabutter, and pour the fudge into it. Give it time to cool until you can shape it with your hands.

4. Coat your hands in butter or water and shape the fudge into spheres. Roll them over the chocolate sprinkles (which should be spread out on a flat plate), chill them, and serve.

WEEDY SONORAN MELCOCHAS

Equipment:

- Medium-Sized Saucepan
- Wooden Spatula
- Cellophane
- Rectangular Glass Baking Dish

Ingredients:

- 1 cup of Water
- 2 cups of Granulated Sugar
- 4 tablespoons of Cannabutter
- ½ teaspoon of Vanilla Extract
- Anise Seeds
- Mint

Procedure:

1. Melt the cannabutter in a saucepan with the water over medium heat. Add sugar and stir until it dissolves.
2. Continue cooking without stirring. Your caramel will begin to bubble and turn into a light golden brown shade.
   *Pro-tip for the right consistency: if you dip a dollop of caramel into a cold glass of water, the caramel should be soft, but still holding its shape. If it is too malleable and spreads, it means the caramel needs more time on the stove.

3. Once the perfect texture is reached, pour the caramel into the greased baking dish and allow

it to cool until you can handle it with your hands.

4. Add the vanilla extract and the mint. Coat your hands in cannabutter, and begin to stretch, fold, and stretch the caramel again as you would with taffy. Knead, and repeat the stretching pattern a few more times. The result should be creamy and almost solid.

5. Cut the melcocha into long bite-sized pieces, sprinkle a few anise seeds, and wrap in cellophane.

Marijuana Halva (Persian Rosewater Candy)

Equipment:

- Medium Saucepan
- Large Saucepan
- Whisk
- Rectangular Glass Baking Dish
- Knife

Ingredients:

- ½ cup of Sugar
- ½ cup of Water
- 4 tablespoons of Rosewater
- 1 thread of Saffron
- ¼ cup of Unsalted Butter
- ¼ cup of Cannabutter
- ¾ cup of All-Purpose Flour

Procedure:

1. Using medium heat, boil the water in the saucepan and dissolve the sugar. Pour the rose-scented water and the thread of saffron (one will be enough to give flavor and color to this sweet) and move away from the stove.

2. Melt both types of butter in the larger of the two pans using low-heat and incorporate the flour– the texture should resemble a paste of sorts.

3. Add the sugary mix into the paste once the latter reaches a golden color (that's our favorite hue in the dessert world), and once again remove the pan from the stove.

4. With your wooden spatula and the baking dish, spread the paste, chill it until it sets, and cut it into whichever shapes you would like.

CANNABIS-INFUSED GERMAN COFFEECAKE

Equipment:

- 9-inch baking pan

- Large Mixing Bowl

- Medium Mixing Bowl

- Small Bowl

- Whisk

Ingredients:

For the cake mix-

- ¾ cup of All-Purpose Flour
- 3 tablespoons of Granulated Sugar
- 3 tablespoons of Brown Sugar
- ¼ teaspoon of Powdered Cinnamon
- A dash of Nutmeg
- A sprinkle of Salt
- ⅓ cup of Milk
- 1 Egg
- ½ teaspoon of Almond Extract
- 2 tablespoons of Melted Cannabis Butter
- 1 cup of berry mixes (raspberries, blueberries, blackberries)

For the Streusel topping-

- 3 tablespoons of Granulated Sugar
- 3 tablespoons of Brown Sugar
- ¼ cup of All-Purpose Flour

- 2 tablespoons of Melted Cannabutter

Instructions:

1. Prepare your 9-inch round cake tin by greasing the sides and the bottom with regular unsalted butter, and lining it with non-stick parchment paper. The oven must be heating up nicely at 345° Fahrenheit.

2. In order to make the batter, sift the flour and gather it along with the sugar, baking powder, cinnamon, nutmeg, and salt into the largest of your bowls.

3. Your medium bowl is the place to whisk together your egg, milk, and almond extract, all of which will be added right into the large bowl with the dry items once they are fully incorporated. Include the melted cannabutter once the batter is halfway uniform.

4. Pour the batter into the cake tin and bang it against the counter a few times, so the top evens out and the air escapes. Plop your berries all over the cake batter in any pattern you desire.*

*Make sure your berries are fresh, washed, and very much dry by the time we get to this step, otherwise there will be air pockets in your cake.

5. Use the final container to make the streusel topping by mixing them all together (first dry ingredients, then wet) and sprinkling the result onto the batter and the berries.

6. Bake the cake for 45 minutes and do the toothpick test for good measure. Once it is ready, and your kitchen is wafting with the scent of warm cake and baked berries, allow your dessert to cool before serving with a scoop of whipped cream (which is optional).

Pun-Intended Baked Cannabis Pudding

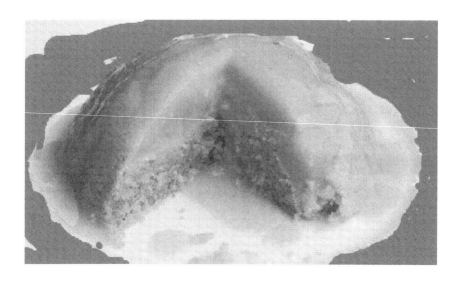

Equipment:

- Large Mixing Bowl
- Two Medium Mixing Bowls
- Whisk
- 8-inch round cake tin
- Medium Saucepan

Ingredients:

For the Bread-Apricot Pudding-

- ¼ cup of Granulated Sugar
- 1 Egg
- ½ cup of All-Purpose Flour
- ½ teaspoon of Baking Soda
- A dash of Salt
- ¼ cup of Milk
- 1 tablespoon of Cannabutter
- ½ tablespoon of Apricot Jam
- ½ tablespoon of Apple Cider Vinegar

For the Sauce-

- ¼ cup of Water
- 4 tablespoons of Unsalted Butter
- ¼ cup of Brown Sugar
- ¼ cup of Heavy Cream
- ¼ cup of Cannabis-Infused Cream
- ½ teaspoon of Vanilla Extract

Procedure:

1. Preheat the oven to 345-° Fahrenheit.

2. Sift the flour, salt, and baking soda in the medium bowl, while using the large bowl to whisk the egg and sugar.

3. Use the second medium-sized bowl to whisk in the melted cannabutter, apricot jam, apple cider vinegar, and milk.

4. Going by the rule of thirds (one-third of dry ingredients into eggs and sugar, one-third of the milk mixture into that, and repeat until the ingredients are all mixed into the largest bowl).

5. For your sauce: In the saucepan, boil water, sugar, and butter. Then move away from the stove and mix in the cannacream, regular cream, and vanilla until you have a bit of a custard-looking mixture.

6. The cake batter should go in the prepared cake tin (greased and lined with parchment paper) and it ought to be baked for 45 minutes, as per the toothpick test.

7. Serve the pudding still warm and pour the sauce on top. Enjoy your baked goods!

CONCLUSION

Several fire extinguishers later, here we are, back in a single piece. On a more serious note, if you stayed with me all throughout this book, I fore mostly wanted to say thank you. I hope you enjoyed it, and I definitely urge you to at least try one of the recipes you saw.

A surprising amount of work went into the project, and although there already are several books and guides on cannabis and cannabis-related recipes, I decided to give this one a more personal type of approach in some parts.

It could turn into a dry subject without the proper care, and it would mean the world if you could post a review on your thoughts about my work.

This could be considered my first attempt at writing a full-scale published piece of my own, and it is rather interesting how the pieces fell to make it happen.

The writing process itself was a learning experience, as I had to do research on this topic including (but not limited to) asking long-term smokers and acquaintances of mine what recipes they would find the most tempting, which processes I should focus on informing the audience about and reading article after article about methods of extraction I had not even heard about before.

While it is not recommended to try every single extraction method (So. Many. Lawsuits), I do recommend trying any or all of the recipes listed. If marijuana is not legally available in your area of residence, you should still try the recipes with regular butter or oil for the mere pleasure of enjoying sugary treats in your free time.

The best part about these desserts is that they taste great regardless of whether they are cannabis-infused or not.

So whether it is for medicinal reasons, or for the simple act of fulfilling a sweet craving in the middle of the night with something a bit more dignified than a spoonful of Nutella (even though we all know that is satisfying as can be), this book is targeted for more than one type of audience.

Thank you for sharing this portion of your time with me, and I hope you have an excellent baking session!

50045142R00062

Made in the USA
San Bernardino, CA
26 August 2019